Shindig

A Play

Arthur Aldrich

A Samuel French Acting Edition

SAMUELFRENCH-LONDON.CO.UK
SAMUELFRENCH.COM

Copyright © 1992 by Samuel French Ltd
All Rights Reserved

SHINDIG is fully protected under the copyright laws of the British Commonwealth, including Canada, the United States of America, and all other countries of the Copyright Union. All rights, including professional and amateur stage productions, recitation, lecturing, public reading, motion picture, radio broadcasting, television and the rights of translation into foreign languages are strictly reserved.

ISBN 978-0-573-03382-7

www.samuelfrench-london.co.uk

www.samuelfrench.com

FOR AMATEUR PRODUCTION ENQUIRIES

UNITED KINGDOM AND WORLD EXCLUDING NORTH AMERICA

plays@SamuelFrench-London.co.uk

020 7255 4302/01

Each title is subject to availability from Samuel French,

depending upon country of performance.

CAUTION: Professional and amateur producers are hereby warned that *SHINDIG* is subject to a licensing fee. Publication of this play does not imply availability for performance. Both amateurs and professionals considering a production are strongly advised to apply to the appropriate agent before starting rehearsals, advertising, or booking a theatre. A licensing fee must be paid whether the title is presented for charity or gain and whether or not admission is charged.

The professional rights in this play are controlled by Samuel French Ltd, 52 Fitzroy Street, London, W1T 5JR.

No one shall make any changes in this title for the purpose of production. No part of this book may be reproduced, stored in a retrieval system, or transmitted in any form, by any means, now known or yet to be invented, including mechanical, electronic, photocopying, recording, videotaping, or otherwise, without the prior written permission of the publisher. No one shall upload this title, or part of this title, to any social media websites.

The right of Arthur Aldrich to be identified as author of this work has been asserted by him in accordance with Section 77 of the Copyright, Designs and Patents Act 1988

SHINDIG

First performed at the Phoenix Arts Centre, Leicester by Oadby Drama Society on 10th June 1990 with the following cast of characters:

Kate Barton	Ivy Berry
Roz Harding	Carol James
Liz Spicer	Jackie Rossa
Julia Roberts	Sally Massey
Barbara Ash	Shan Hughes

Directed by John Dexter

SETTING

The action takes place in the inner sanctum of the typing pool attached to the Sales Office of Harrison Hosiery Ltd.

There are two doors, one UR opening into a corridor, and one DL leading into the main typing pool. A window C, overlooks the factory yard.

There are four desks, complete with typists' chairs and typewriters. Kate's desk is DR; the three arranged in a line L belong to Roz, Barbara and Liz.

There are coat pegs on the wall next to the door R and a filing cabinet upstage between the door and Kate's desk.

The office is festively decorated — streamers, a Christmas tree and cards on every available surface.

Time — the present. Thursday and Friday immediately before Christmas

Also by Arthur Aldrich published
by Samuel French Ltd

The Road To Northborough

SHINDIG

Scene 1

It is 8.50 on the Thursday morning before Christmas

Kate Barton, mature and formidable, is seated at her desk UR, *opening the morning's mail with a knife. She removes the letters from the envelopes and sorts them into three piles*

The door R *opens and Roz Harding, mature but not formidable, enters*

Roz 'Morning, Kate. (*She removes her coat and hangs it up beside the door*)
Kate Welcome! I was just beginning to feel very lonely.
Roz Where would they be without us old troopers?
Kate Up the creek without a paddle and serve them bloody right.
Roz (*crossing to her desk* L *and sitting*) What's the news?
Kate Lesley's husband just rang. She's got it now.
Roz Not surprised. She was showing all the signs.
Kate Which means I've got to look after next door as well as this place. Same every Christmas. Always a flu epidemic. How I long for something original, like German Measles. Still, ties in nicely with their last minute shopping. (*She holds out a letter*) One for you!
Roz (*crossing to collect it*) Who can that be?
Kate I wonder if Barbara'll be in today? She didn't look too good yesterday.

Roz (*opening the envelope*) She was sick in the ladies.
Kate Really?
Roz Said it must be something she ate. (*She reads the Christmas card*) It's from Deirdre. You remember Deirdre. Left ... oh about eighteen months ago to have a baby.
Kate Has she had it yet?

The door R opens and Liz Spicer, sexy and glamorous, enters

Roz I think so. Yes, yes ... she must have, silly.
Kate 'Morning, Liz! Welcome back!
Liz Thanks a bundle. (*She hangs up her coat*) 'Morning, Roz.
Roz Better are we?
Liz (*crossing to her desk L*) Was when I got out of bed. Not so bloody sure after thirty minutes on a corporation bus.
Kate You'll be pleased to know you weren't alone. There were six away yesterday.
Liz Doesn't please me at all. I wouldn't wish what I had on my worst enemy.

Julia Roberts, young and bright, enters R in a rush. She hangs up her coat

Julia 'Morning.

Julia rushes out again

Liz 'Morn—— What's the matter with her?
Roz Perhaps she needs the loo.
Kate Forgotten to collect the sales invoices more like.
Liz Poor kid always looks scared out of her wits.
Roz A bit of fear never did a junior any harm.

Shindig

Barbara Ash, quiet and attractive, enters R

Barbara (*taking off her coat and hanging it up*) G'morning, Kate. G'morning, Roz.
Roz How are you today?
Barbara Fine thanks. (*To Liz who is staring at her*) 'Morning.
Roz Of course you two've never met, have you?
Liz No. (*She holds out her hand*) I'm Liz.

They shake hands

Barbara Barbara. I've heard a lot about you.
Liz And I thought it was the flu making my ears burn.
Roz I keep thinking I'm about to go down with it.
Kate Not you, Roz! You've done your shopping.
Liz One day, Kate, one day ...
Kate What?
Liz We all know how fit and healthy you are.
Kate Mind over matter.
Liz I could almost wish you a dose of flu, just to dent your complacency. (*She searches in the filing tray on her desk*) Now, just as a matter of interest, did anyone finish my letters for Andy Peters?
Kate What letters?
Liz A couple of letters he gave me before I went to do my Christmas shopping.
Kate Fat chance!
Liz That's nice.
Kate There isn't anyone in the pool can read your shorthand for a start.
Roz Don't worry, Liz, Andrew went down with the flu same time as you.
Liz (*smiling*) Really? In that case — (*she picks up her shorthand*

notebook) — I think I'll go and see if he's better. (*She moves to the door* R)
Kate Don't be long! There's still plenty to do.
Liz Just re-establish my credentials.

As Liz opens the door

Julia returns at speed with a filing tray containing papers

She and Liz almost collide

Ay up, kid!
Julia Sorry! Sorry!
Liz Slow down! It's only work.

Liz exits R

Julia crosses to Kate's desk

Roz Poison!
Kate Pardon?
Roz The new perfume. Liz is wearing it. It's called ——
Kate (*interrupting*) Poison! Very appropriate.
Julia Sales invoices, Miss Barton.
Kate (*taking the tray*) Is this all?
Julia Mr Gardiner said ——
Kate (*interrupting*) I know ... (*Deep voice*) The bottom's fallen out of sales, Miss Roberts.
Julia Yes, that's right.
Kate (*deep voice*) I blame Christmas.
Julia Very good!
Kate (*normal voice*) Years of practice, girl. All right, leave 'em with me. You'd better start on the filing.

Shindig

Julia Yes ...*(She starts to go out* L*)*
Barbara 'Morning, Julia.
Julia 'Morning, Mrs ... er ... Ash.
Barbara The name's Barbara. I did tell you.
Julia Yes. Sorry!

Julia exits L

Kate Of course we all know why Liz has come back.
Roz Oh yes, the office party! Like a moth to the flame.
Barbara That's tomorrow, surely?
Kate Today to sow the seed. Tomorrow to reap the harvest. I was hoping she'd stay away altogether.
Roz How are you on office parties, Barbara?
Barbara I've been to a few.
Kate But nothing quite like the Sales Office Christmas shindig, I bet?
Barbara Bit riotous, is it?
Kate It's a contradiction in terms for a start. Not what Christmas is about.
Roz Some of those sales clerks get ... well ...
Kate Pissed is the word you're looking for, Roz.
Roz Some of the girls are as bad.
Kate Which brings us nicely back to Liz Spicer. *(She stands)* Well ... I suppose I'd better take a roll call next door. You could make a start on the invoices.
Roz Rightio.

Kate goes out L

Roz checks through the invoices on Kate's desk

You mustn't mind Kate.

Barbara I don't.
Roz She's good-hearted really.
Barbara Doesn't seem very fond of Liz.
Roz Oh the sparks fly there sometimes. She doesn't approve of Liz. Well I don't either. I don't know any woman who does. (*She returns to her own desk with the invoices which she proceeds to divide into three piles*)
Barbara Why's that?
Roz Oh, I mustn't say things. You make up your own mind. (*Slight pause*) What it boils down to, I suppose, is sex appeal. Liz has so much, she makes everyone else feel as if they haven't got any.
Barbara Oh well ... good luck to her!
Roz That's not what most people say. (*She gives the invoices to Barbara*) That's your little lot. Not going to be rushed off our feet today.

Barbara opens her desk drawer and takes out a pad of blank invoices

Roll on Christmas.
Barbara Yes.
Roz I must admit, I'm really looking forward to the holiday.
Barbara Me too!
Roz Have you made any plans?
Barbara Oh yes! I'm going away, actually. For the first time in my life, I'm spending Christmas in a hotel.
Roz How lovely! Just you and your husband?
Barbara No ... no husband ... I'm divorced.
Roz Sorry, I didn't realize.
Barbara Just me and the boyfriend. It's no great secret. You may as well know ... he's coming to live with me after Christmas.
Roz New start then! Do I hear wedding bells?

Barbara (*with a laugh*) Not unless your hearing's better than mine.
Roz I hope ... I hope you're over your sickness in time for the hotel ... and Christmas.
Barbara Oh that ... yes, no problem.
Roz You haven't told Kate ...?
Barbara About the boyfriend? No! If she doesn't approve of Liz, I stand no chance.
Roz Oh but you're different.
Barbara No ... much the same really. Looking after number one. It's the only way nowadays. My big mistake first time round. I was so unselfish. I hardly existed.
Roz A lot of women don't. I mean, I don't at home. Very quiet. You'd hardly recognize me.
Barbara Is Liz married?
Roz Yes. Kevin Spicer ... works in the Council offices. Happily married. In fact she's probably the happiest married person in the whole of the Sales Office. Ironic, isn't it!

Liz enters R as Roz is speaking

Liz What's ironic?
Roz That was quick.
Liz A lightning tour of the troops. I do wonders for their morale. They don't do a bad job on mine either. Everyone's looking forward to the party.

Liz sits at her typewriter, takes out paper and carbons from the desk drawer, collates them and puts them into the typewriter

So, how are you settling in, love?
Barbara Oh ... fine thanks. I like it here.
Liz Where's ...? (*She indicates Kate's desk*)

Barbara Next door.
Liz Changing the nappies or putting up new Jason and Kylie posters?
Barbara Something like that.

They all type for a few moments

Liz (*stops typing*) I know where it was.
Barbara (*also stopping*) Sorry?
Liz I saw you last week-end. I've just remembered where. It was in Whittaker's.
Barbara Oh yes.
Liz Enjoy your meal?
Barbara Yes, thanks. Did you?
Liz I work there, love. Behind the bar.
Roz (*stops typing*) I thought you had the flu.
Liz Last Friday I was better. On Sunday I had a relapse. All right?
Roz I thought it might be something like that.
Liz You were with Malcolm Clark.
Barbara (*glancing at Roz*) Yes.
Roz What ... our Malcolm Clark?
Liz I thought, who's the lucky lady? Now I know.
Roz Oh dear! Oh dear! (*She resumes typing, shaking her head*)
Liz You're a fast worker.
Barbara Pardon?
Liz Only here a fortnight! Oh, for God's sake, Roz, if you want to lay an egg, lay it!
Barbara I've known him for nearly a year. He helped me get the job here.
Liz Ah ... That explains it.

Julia enters L clutching two letters

Julia I'm sorry. I wanted Miss Barton.
Roz She won't be long.
Julia I'll come back. (*She goes to leave*)
Liz (*intercepting her*) Eh ... eh, Miss Perpetual Motion, slow down! There's no law against waiting.
Julia No, but ...
Liz Sit! (*She indicates Kate's chair*)
Julia I can't sit there. Suppose Miss Barton ——
Liz (*pushing her into the chair*) Sit down! So, Julia, the thousand dollar question is ... what are you and me going to wear for the party tomorrow?
Julia I dunno ... I ... er ...
Liz You have to dress up, girl. It's a big occasion.
Julia What, you mean fancy dress?
Liz Now there's a thought.
Roz (*stops typing*) No, Julia ... Not fancy dress. Just your best party frock.
Julia Oh, I see.
Liz Tight and sexy, or loose and comfortable? That's the real question.
Roz Wear jeans and a floppy sweater. Give the rest of us a chance.
Liz I'm talking about underwear.
Roz Oh, you wear that as well, do you?
Liz Congratulations, Roz. You sound more like Kate every day.
Barbara Do we have the party in here?
Liz No. In the main office. More room.
Barbara So who comes? Just us and the girls next door?
Roz Oh no. There's a goodly selection of men.
Liz More motley than goodly I'd say. But then, we wouldn't want them goodly, would we?
Roz The area salesmen come in for a conference tomorrow morning and stay on for the party.

Liz They think the girls in the pool are their Christmas bonus.

Liz and Barbara laugh

Roz Oh no. Most of them are real gentlemen.
Julia What ... what happens ... at the party?

The interruption takes them by surprise. They all look at her

Liz Pleasure is what happens at parties, young Julia. And in this hell hole that is something to be treasured.
Julia What I meant was ... what do you do?
Roz We have a drink or two and ... er ... sing carols.
Liz Good God, do we?
Roz Wish each other a Merry Christmas, and all go home.
Liz I remember the wishing Merry Christmas bit. But I must've been otherwise engaged during the carols. Are you sure?
Roz Positive!
Julia So there's no dancing then?
Roz Dancing?
Julia Yeah ... we always dance at parties.
Liz No ... well ... not dancing as such. Fred brings in his tape recorder for background music but——
Julia Funny sort of party!
Roz The men aren't interested in dancing.
Liz But do feel free to try, Julia. If you can get old man Levers up off his sit-upon, I'll do the dance of the seven veils.
Julia (*with a smile*) Is that a promise?
Liz Yes. But no chance! The only thing that gloomy old git'll stand up for is the National Anthem.
Roz There's always Max Stone. He enjoys dancing. (*She laughs*)
Julia I don't know him.
Roz Admin Manager, Birmingham office.

Shindig 11

Liz Commonly known as the octopus. His hands breed once a year. Last year it was four pairs, all living happily in the land of the grope.
Roz Two years ago I slapped his face.
Liz Really? Momentous news, Roz. I wonder what he did to deserve that.
Barbara Sounds more like an orgy than a party.
Roz No, we mustn't give the wrong impression. Most of them behave very well, really.
Liz Yes, don't worry, Julia. All good, clean fun.
Julia I'm not worried.

The telephone on Kate's desk rings. Julia stands up immediately

Liz Well answer it, kid!
Julia (*picking up the receiver*) Er ... hallo ...? Pardon? ... Julia Roberts ... Right, yes. (*She giggles, then holds out the receiver*) It's Mr Clark. For you, Liz
Liz Oh, right! (*She crosses and takes the receiver*)

Barbara suddenly becomes very busy with her typing. Roz also reacts, becoming tense

Hallo, Malcolm! What can I do for you? ... Well, we are rather busy ... What about the new secretary?... Barbara, of course. I'm sure she'd happily—— OK. OK. I'm coming. (*She replaces the receiver*) He wants a letter doing.
Roz You've a nerve.
Liz Peace, comrade. I just thought ...(*She picks up her notebook and pencil*)
Barbara Don't worry on my account. I shall see plenty of him over Christmas.
Liz (*laughing*) Aren't you the lucky one!

Liz goes out R

Julia It says on Mr Clark's door that he's the Marketing Development Manager. That's an important job, isn't it! But he's not very old. I think he's ever so attractive.
Roz (*interrupting*) Julia, you'd better go back to your own office. I'll tell Miss Barton you're looking for her.
Julia OK.

Julia goes towards the door L *as Kate enters* R

Kate Yes, Julia, what can I do for you?

Kate crosses to her desk. Julia joins her. Roz and Barbara start typing again

Julia It's about these letters.
Kate What about them?
Julia (*handing the letters to Kate*) They're marked Manchester.
Kate Yes?
Julia But they're not. I mean ... they seem to be Leeds.
Kate Then use your initiative, girl. Cross out Manchester and write Leeds.
Julia I didn't like to ... it being your writing.
Kate Two of my deliberate mistakes, Julia. Did you find the others?
Julia What others?
Kate I'm sure I made more than two. You'd better go and look, hadn't you!
Julia But I've done the rest of the filing.
Kate Then you'll have to undo it.
Julia Oh hell! (*She turns away and immediately turns back*) Can

I ask you something, Miss Barton?
Kate If you must.
Julia This office party. Can I bring my boyfriend?
Kate No, of course you can't. We don't bring guests. Where would it end?
Julia In that case I don't want to come.
Kate Don't want to come? But you'll be here already. Are you listening to this, Roz?
Roz (*stops typing*) Julia, everyone goes to the office party. It's no big deal.
Julia Tell that to my boyfriend!

Julia turns away and hurries out L

Kate (*calling after her*) Julia, wait a minute! Come back! What's the matter with her?
Barbara I think she's got the wrong idea about your office party.
Kate I hope you haven't been frightening her with stories of young sales clerks running riot!
Roz But they do run riot.
Kate Last year, yes. Too much drink and perfume — went to their heads. Good Lord, one of them even tried to kiss me. Well things'll be different this year.
Roz Tell Liz! She's the one who encourages them.

The telephone rings. Kate answers it

Kate Kate Barton speaking ... Oh yes, Mr Levers.... Yes, certainly ...! Yes, on my way. (*She replaces the receiver and stands*) Old misery guts wants to see me.
Roz More complaints?
Kate Probably! Where's Liz?
Roz She's doing a letter for Malcolm Clark.

Kate I hope that's not starting up again.
Roz No. No, of course not!
Kate Birds of a feather those two.

Kate goes out R

Barbara What did that mean?
Roz Nothing! Kate ... well, she gets funny ideas — particularly about Liz.
Barbara Did Liz and Malcolm have an affair?
Roz Don't ask me! Ask them!
Barbara OK. Doesn't bother me. What's past is past.
Roz Yes. You young people seem to have no difficulty wiping out bits of the past you've finished with — like marriage vows and faithfulness.
Barbara Don't needle me, Roz. I'm not looking for a row.
Roz I don't suppose you know Helen Clark.
Barbara I haven't met her. But Malcolm talks about her quite a lot.
Roz I wonder what she thinks about the past.
Barbara It's over, Roz. I'm not breaking up a happy marriage, if that's what you think.
Roz I couldn't believe my ears when Liz said about you and him. Helen used to work here. It's where he met her. She and I were good friends.
Barbara I'm sure she's a lovely lady. I'd probably like her a lot. But don't ask me to feel sorry for her, or guilty. Malcolm and I are going to live together because both our marriages are finished and we love one another.
Roz His marriage has been finished a few times to my knowledge.
Barbara It won't work. I won't be scared away by what happened in the past, either between him and Liz or him and

anyone else. We're going to have a marvellous Christmas together, and we're going to be very happy.

Roz Time someone made Malcolm Clark happy.

Barbara I will, don't worry. I intend to work very hard at it. When I think of the mistakes I made — we both made — first time round. No love, no respect and no dignity! God forbid life ever gets like that again. You see, that's why I can't afford to ignore this chance; can't let it be spoilt by feelings of guilt. And I'm sorry if that offends you.

Roz Yes ... dignity! Very important! Went out of my marriage a few years back.

Barbara What happened?

Roz If you must know, someone ... someone borrowed my husband. When he came back, I couldn't be the same person he left. Nowadays people still borrow him — like a library book. He always comes back.

Barbara Roz, you shouldn't stand for ——

Roz (*interrupting sharply*) Don't tell me what I should and shouldn't stand for! I've done nothing to be ashamed of. That's what keeps me going. But I'll give you some advice. Don't let on to Liz how much in love you are. It's a challenge she can't resist.

Barbara Liz seems all right. Why do you hate her so much?

Roz I hate what she represents. One day she'll be cut down to size. I shall enjoy that. (*She gets up and moves towards the door* R. *Turning*) Does he know about your morning sickness?

Barbara No ... I mean, it wasn't anything.

Roz You don't fool me.

Barbara Well ... I thought I'd tell him at Christmas.

Roz Your decision! I just hope you're not too late.

Roz goes out R

Barbara sits looking concerned as the Lights fade to Black-out

SCENE 2

Early afternoon, the following day

The Lights comes up on Liz, in her finery, blowing up balloons with a pump. Kate, looking smart rather than partyish, is sitting at her desk going through a tray of filing, stamping each piece of paper with a rubber stamp. There are glasses on Liz's desk and a pile of blown-up balloons on Barbara's desk

Pause, as Liz pumps and Kate stamps

Liz I suppose you didn't warn young Julia about balloons?
Kate Never mentioned 'em.
Liz Something must've frightened her away.
Kate You, painting lurid pictures of the office party, that's what frightened her away.
Liz (*tying up the neck of the balloon and disconnecting the pump*) I never did. I paint the town occasionally. But pictures? No!(*She adds the balloon to the pile*) Well, that's your lot! I shall now conserve my energy for better things. (*She takes a bottle of Martini from her desk drawer*)
Kate (*opening a letter with her knife*) One of them's gone down already. (*She points*)
Liz What? Where? (*She looks at the heap from Kate's point of view*) Oh hell! (*Pulling out a sad and deflated balloon*) Reminds me of something. Can't quite think what. (*She discards the balloon and opens the bottle of Martini*)
Kate Barbara's a long time.
Liz Closeted with Malcolm Clark.
Kate What's that all about?
Liz (*pouring two drinks*) Not work, that's for sure.

Kate Perhaps I ought to warn her about Malcolm Clark.
Liz Bit late for that. (*She gives Kate a glass*) Cheers!
Kate Oh yes ... Happy Christmas!

They drink

I suppose you wouldn't like to put me in the picture.
Liz I imagine they're sorting out a little misunderstanding — like she thinks she's going to spend Christmas with him.
Kate Where did she get that idea from?
Liz She also thinks that she and Malcolm are going to live together. Well, we all know Malcolm. Lovely fellow, always good for a slap and tickle.
Kate Speak for yourself.
Liz I am. As he said to me ... How could he possibly leave Helen after ten happy years? In other words, he doesn't have the guts.
Kate What's your involvement?
Liz For once, Kate, no involvement. Just a shoulder to cry on.

The door R opens and Julia enters. She is wearing an attractive skirt and blouse and sporting a very nasty black eye

If it isn't Julia. Good God, girl, what on earth ...?
Julia Sorry I wasn't in this morning, Miss Barton. Mum wanted me to stay at home.
Kate What have you been up to?
Julia Nothing!
Liz What does the other chap look like?
Julia Is there anything for me to do?
Kate Julia, love, what happened?
Julia It was my boyfriend, if you must know.
Liz You don't want to stand for that, kid.
Julia My ex-boyfriend. He didn't want me to go to the office

party. When I told him I had to go, he said to pretend to be ill.
Kate Oh, how pathetic!
Julia He stood there shouting at me and that made my mind up. I did want to go. Then he hit me.
Kate I hope you've been to the police.
Julia No! He didn't mean to do it. He cried afterwards. But that's it, isn't it. I couldn't stay with him after that.
Liz Good for you, Julia!
Julia So, is there anything I can do to help?
Kate Are you sure you want to be seen at the party with a shiner like that?
Julia Doesn't matter! I'm going to enjoy myself. That's what it's all about, isn't it, Liz?
Liz Sure is! Enjoying yourself! Number one priority. Here, have a drink! (*She pours a glass of Martini*)
Julia Thanks. In any case, I promised to help with the music.
Kate Music? What music?
Julia Music to dance to.
Kate Not all that — what's it called — Acid House?
Julia Jumbo ... er ... Mr Bates says there'll be something for everyone.
Kate Well tell him I want Beethoven's Pastoral Symphony.

The door L opens and Roz enters, also smartly — and expensively — dressed. She has been imbibing

Roz The lads want to know how long you'll be with the balloons.
Liz Bloody cheek!
Roz Hallo, Julia. I thought you had the flu. (*She goes close to her*) Jumbo was asking after you.
Kate That's a job you can do when you've finished your drink, Julia. Take the balloons across to the Sales Office.
Julia Rightio!

Roz Oh ... Have we started drinking already? How very civilized!
Liz (*holding up the bottle*) It's Dry Martini. Would you care for ——
Roz Lovely! I have to be honest, I've had two very small sherries already.
Liz (*pouring a drink*) In that case, have a very small Martini to go with them.
Roz (*taking the drink*) And a Happy Christmas to you too, Liz. (*She swallows the drink in one gulp*) Now then, Julia, drink up! And I'll give you a hand with these balloons.

Kate takes two polythene sacks from her desk drawer

Kate You can carry them in these.
Julia (*taking the sacks*) Oh, right! (*She quickly empties her glass*)
Roz One for me!

Roz takes a sack from Julia, shakes it open and starts stuffing balloons into it. Julia joins her. Roz whispers to Julia. Julia giggles

Kate And there should be another two dozen next door.

Roz bursts a balloon

Liz Oi, go easy! It took me hours to pump that lot up.
Roz Julia ... Bit heavy on the eye make-up, weren't you!
Julia Pardon?
Roz Your eye make-up. Bit of a mess!
Julia Oh yes ... right! (*She giggles*)

Liz laughs

Roz I've just met Mr Rolfe from Manchester.
Liz Old Randy Rolfe? Yeah, he does a nice line in sherry.
Roz We had a most interesting conversation.
Liz I could tell you a few stories about Randy——

She breaks off as

Barbara enters R. She is also in her best dress but looks tense and unhappy. In silence she crosses to her desk and sits

Roz Come along, young Julia, let's go and see Jumbo Bates about the music. Very important. And you can tell me all about that eye.

Roz and Julia, carrying a sack each, go out L, giggling to one another

Kate (*calling after them*) Don't forget the ones next door. She's drunk before we even start.
Liz It's desperation. Not knowing where the next stiff man's coming from.
Kate (*sharply*) Cut that out!
Liz Sorry, I'm sure. (*She holds out the bottle*) Want a drink, Barbara?
Barbara No! No, thanks.
Kate (*looking at her watch*) Time to blow the whistle, I think.
Liz You mean I can put the cover on my typewritter?
Kate (*moving to the door L*) That'll be the day when you cover anything up. (*She turns back*) By the way, a word of warning. Young Julia's up to something.
Liz Giving make-up lessons is she?
Kate A lot of giggling going on. That always means trouble. (*She opens the door L and calls out*) Right, you lot! Clear your desks!

Kate exits

Liz You have to laugh, don't you!

Slight pause

Well crying ain't no bloody good. (*She pours herself another drink*) Are you sure you won't?
Barbara (*fumbling in her handbag*) Got my own somewhere. (*She takes out a half bottle of gin*)

Liz passes her a glass. Barbara tries to open the bottle but cannot break the seal

Liz Here, let me! (*She undoes the bottle with ease and gives it back to Barbara*) I wouldn't've taken you for a gin drinker.

Barbara pours herself a large gin

Eh, go easy, girl! That's powerful medicine.
Barbara (*raising her glass*) Happy Christmas! (*She takes a long drink*)
Liz Yeah, why not! (*She also drinks*)
Barbara (*finally*) What's going on between you and Malcolm?
Liz Between me and any man, a few electric shocks, occasional big bang. Smoke clears. Nothing left.
Barbara He said you were just good friends.
Liz Men make assumptions like that. I tell 'em — don't count your chickens!
Barbara We've just had the most awful row. We were going to spend Christmas together. He says I imagined it. Why?
Liz Misunderstanding, I suppose.

Barbara I know what he promised.
Liz Well ... He's a very weak man.
Barbara Yes, he is, isn't he! I hadn't realized.
Liz He's no loss!
Barbara But I love him.
Liz Ah well ... Don't know much about love. Went there once and got hurt.
Barbara Christmas, two years ago, that was when our marriage died ... Me and Brian. Two days of rows. And then the silence. That was the worst part, the silence. This was to be the Christmas to wipe out all the bad memories. (*Slight pause*) What am I going to do?
Liz Come and spend Christmas with me and Kevin.
Barbara Pardon?
Liz Christmas Day, Boxing Day ... Be pleased to have you around.
Barbara No ... No I couldn't.
Liz I promise you, no rows! And definitely no silence!
Barbara What's he like?
Liz Kevin? Big, soft. And a lovely friend.
Barbara Is that enough?
Liz It's all we expect of one another. Look, we never ask questions, so we never tell lies. He doesn't sit at home moping, you know. He's got his own office party. It's the only time he wears his black G string. What am I supposed to make of that?
Barbara His what?
Liz G string. You know ... Nut bag. For his banana and apples. Bloody painful I should think, so he must be wearing it for a reason.
Barbara How could I be so blind? Oh God, I've made a right mess of it. I mean, I was so sure of him.
Liz You haven't done anything silly, have you? (*Slight pause*) Like getting pregnant?

Pause. Barbara doesn't answer

Oh Jesus, that's no way to have an affair. Where's the pleaseure in that?
Barbara I wanted a baby. That's how sure I was of him.
Liz Don't we all — at the right time. Still, no problem nowadays. Get him to treat you to a good clinic.
Barbara What are you on about?
Liz Termination, love.
Barbara (*crying out*) No!
Liz He'll know who to contact. He's had to do it before.
Barbara No.
Liz All over in a couple of hours. Best way in the circumstances. When things are different ... Well ... Plenty more where that came from.
Barbara He said that. What a lot you seem to have in common.
Liz You make him pay, love. Get him sorted!

The door L opens and Julia, now wearing a party hat enters in a rush. There is a snatch of pop music as the door opens

Julia Liz! Liz, we're ready to start dancing ... (*She stops*) Oh, sorry!
Barbara Take her away, Julia.
Liz Dancing is it?
Julia Well ... Music anyway. They'll probably start dancing when you come.
Liz Too right they bloody will. What about old man Levers?
Julia I didn't think I'd bother him after all.
Liz No ... He's a tough nut, Julia. Go on! Along in a sec.
Julia You as well, Barbara. This'll be good fun.

Julia goes out L. Snatch of pop music

Liz No point in sitting moping, Barbara. Come and have a few drinks. Take your mind off——
Barbara (*interrupting*) You go on! I'll ... er ...
Liz (*moving to the door* L; *turning back*) You think I interfered between you and Malcolm, but honestly I didn't. I do know he's not for you ... You deserve better than that. Look, where you are, I've been there. But I escaped and I swore "never again!" There's no-one can hurt me now. I'm free. You can escape as well, love. Don't forget ... Christmas Day at my place. We'll have fun.

Liz goes out L. A snatch of music as the door opens and closes

Barbara sits for a moment, staring into space. Then she tops up her glass. From her handbag she takes a Christmas card, opens and reads it. Then, in a fit of anger, she tears it across and drops it on her desk

She stands, picks up her drink and moves across the office, deep in thought. She picks up the letter-opening knife from Kate's desk and moves away with it, weighing it in her hand, as if contemplating its use

The door L *opens, with accompanying music, and Kate enters, carrying a white envelope*

Kate (*with some glee*) Now is the woodcock near the gin.
Barbara It's mine. I was going to bring it to the party.
Kate (*searching on her desk*) Not that sort of gin. Shakespeare! The only bit I ever remember. Gin is a trap and a woodcock is a bird. And our bird is near the trap.

Barbara I'm not with you.
Kate (*taking the knife from Barbara*) That's what I'm looking for. (*She opens her Christmas card*) Young Liz is about to fall into the trap. Julia will ask Mr Levers to dance, and I have it on good authority that he'll dance. A thousand voices will then demand that Liz does the dance of the seven veils. With a bit of luck it should be the last dance she ever does in this place. Never could understand why every office party has to turn into a sexual tango. Spoils everything. But just this once, if it cuts that bird of paradise down to size, then it's OK by me. (*She takes the card out of the envelope*) Ah, that's nice! A Christmas card from the Chairman. He always sends me one. At least someone appreciates my efforts to keep this office ticking over efficiently. You've no idea what a strain it can be sometimes.

Barbara turns suddenly, picks up the gin bottle, and goes out R

(*Turning*) Would you like to see the card?

The door slams

Oh! Oh sugar! What's going on with you, lass?

She sees the torn Christmas card on Barbara's desk, picks it up and pieces it together. She shakes her head and drops the card back on the desk

Haven't the brains they were born with!

Shaking her head in disbelief at everyone else's stupidity, she moves back to her own desk. She sits, reads the Chairman's card again and then stands it up beside her typewriter

The door L opens and Liz enters slamming it behind her. The noises off during the few seconds the door is open are of pop music and baying male voices

Liz Oh ... Might've known you'd be here.
Kate Wouldn't miss it for the world, dear. Unless, of course, you're going to run away home.
Liz Where's Barbara?
Kate Gone to the loo, I think.
Liz (*sitting at her desk*) Stupid! Stupid! Stupid!
Kate I take it Mr Levers is dancing.
Liz Like a great fat whale with a silly grin on his face.
Kate Are you surprised?
Liz You knew, I suppose.
Kate I warned you.
Liz This isn't fun. It's revenge. You and Roz! And you tricked Julia into helping.
Kate It just so happens that old man Levers is Julia's uncle.
Liz (*amused*) You what?
Kate Bit of a surprise, eh!
Liz Cheeky little toe rag! Please, Uncle, may I have this dance? And then Liz will take off all her clothes. (*She laughs*)

The door L opens and Roz and Julia enter. The same noises offstage

Roz There she is!
Liz Is that a riot I hear out there?
Julia I'm sorry, Liz. I didn't think they'd be like that.
Liz Little lesson for you, kid. Men are animals. Ought to be kept in cages.
Roz I thought you were the one who could handle them.

Liz Enjoying yourself, Roz?
Roz I could go and tell them you've gone home.

Pause

Liz Like hell! Have you ever seen so many men bulging at the seams? I can't disappoint my fan club, can I?
Kate Liz, I don't know what you're intending to do, but forget it! It'll get out of hand.
Liz I don't welch on promises, Kate. And I can handle it. Now what do we use for seven veils?
Julia Look, I can say it was all a joke. You don't need——
Liz (*interrupting*) You got that black eye from a man. Let's say that this is my revenge for your black eye.
Julia I don't follow.
Liz Balloons! Will you settle for balloons?
Julia It isn't ...
Liz The dance of the seven balloons. Seven little pricks and they're all gone. Julia, go and fetch Barbara. You'll find her in the loo. This'll be for her as well. Go on!

Julia goes out R

Roz, perhaps you'd like to fetch me seven assorted balloons.
Roz With pleasure. The smallest I can find.

Roz exits L. *Same noises off stage*

Liz She's enjoying herself. And all because I kissed her husband under the misletoe.
Kate And the rest.
Liz One thing leads to another. I felt sorry for the dried-up old stick. Now then, Kate, are you an expert on Arabian dances?

Shall I strip to the buff? Or shall I keep my stockings on to create an air of mystery?

Kate You go ahead with this and you'll lose your job. I'll guarantee it.

Liz Think I care? Besides, the only people who can sack me are out there with their tongues hanging out. By the time I've finished, they'll be the ones with the red faces. It'll be their jobs on the line, their marriages and their futures.

The door R opens and Julia rushes in

Julia (*slightly hysterical*) Liz ... Miss Barton ... Please ... Help!

Liz What's the matter?

Julia Quick ... you must come ...!

Liz (*raising her voice*) What is it?

Julia Please ... It's Barbara!

Kate Oh God, now what?

Liz (*taking Julia by the shoulders*) Calm down, girl! Where is she?

Julia In the ladies ... There's blood everywhere. She's ... She's lying ... (*She covers her face with her hands*)

Liz Kate, get Sally!

Kate Who?

Liz Sally Rimmer — she's the First Aider. (*She pulls Julia into a chair*) You stay here, Julia. (*She picks up the telephone receiver and thrusts it into Kate's hand*) Wake up, Kate!

Liz runs out R

Kate puts the receiver to her ear. Julia sits shaking and upset

Kate As if we didn't have enough problems. (*She dials a three digit number*) What has she done?

No answer from Julia

Julia! What has she done?
Julia I don't know. There's a broken bottle ... She's cut—all up her arm. It's ... It's awful ...

Roz enters L, *clutching seven balloons of various shapes and sizes, strung together for easy handling. There is a burst of loud music until the door is closed*

Roz Right then, where's Salome?
Kate (*into the telephone*) Sally? It's Kate ... yes, and to you! Listen, your services are required ... Your First Aid services, of course ... Second floor toilet, one of my girls——
Roz What's going on?
Kate — I'm not absolutely sure what .. but ... er ... you'd better take some Elastoplast ... No, no, not Alka Seltzer. (*Shouting*) Elastoplast ...! No, thank *you*! (*She slams down the receiver*) The party obviously started early in Accounts.
Roz Would someone mind telling me what's happened?
Kate Barbara! Silly idiot's cut her wrists.
Roz God, no!
Kate Isn't that right, Julia?
Julia She was just lying there, on the floor. I slipped in the ... There's blood all over her clothes.
Roz (*discarding the balloons*) There, there, love! (*She puts her arms round Julia*) Don't upset yourself! Well, who'd've thought she'd do a thing like that?
Kate I don't know. I give up.
Roz Of course she does have problems ...
Kate If everyone who's got problems did that, there'd be no-one left.
Roz No. (*Slight pause*) Where's Liz?

Julia She's gone to help.
Roz You realize what this means, don't you!
Kate It means someone's going to have a mess to clear up.
Roz She's escaped. We had her at our mercy and she's wriggled out of it.
Kate There'll also be a lot of questions and a lot of pointing fingers — mostly at me, if I know anything.
Roz She's ruined the party.
Kate Oh yes, she's done that all right.
Julia (*breaking from Roz. Shouting*) Be quiet! How can you talk like that?

Slight pause

Kate Liz will need help.
Roz Don't look at me. I'm not dressed for playing nurses.
Kate Ah well, I suppose muggins will do it. And Julia, pull yourself together! It's only an accident and life's littered with them.
Roz What about next door?
Kate Leave 'em! Let them blow themselves out.
Roz It was going to be——
Kate (*interrupting*) Forget it!

Liz enters R. Julia runs to her

Julia Liz, is she ...?
Liz Is she what? (*She puts her arm round Julia*) Well, she's not laughing her head off, kid. But she'll survive.
Kate Thank God for that!
Liz Actually, thank Gladys!
Kate Gladys who?

Liz Gladys the tea lady. Seems she was a nurse once upon a time. She just took over—did everything. I didn't even get my hands dirty. But I did sacrifice one stocking in the cause of medical science.
Kate Pardon?
Liz Ideal for a tourniquet, according to Gladys. Well, it was the least I could do.
Kate I thought Sally Rimmer would have that sort of thing.
Liz Sally? Pissed as a newt! Took one look at the mess and was sick into the toilet. No ... Gladys is your man.
Julia Are you sure she'll be all right?
Liz Gladys says so. All organized. Ambulance on its way. Nothing else to do, so I thought I'd come back and entertain the troops. Then I realized— only one stocking. Can't do a strip-tease improperly dressed, can I? Sorry, Roz.
Roz You think you've escaped, don't you!
Liz I know I have. After all, one word from me and Jumbo takes his music home.
Roz Why would he do that?
Liz Because he owes me— that's why. In fact quite a lot of them owe me. On the other hand, nobody owes you anything, do they, Roz?
Roz No! And I'm proud of it.
Liz Good for you! (*She picks up the balloons*) Anyway, I won't be needing these now. (*She picks up Kate's letter knife and "gently" bursts six of the seven balloons*) Such pretty colours too! Here you are, Roz! One for you! (*She puts the knife and remaining balloon on Roz's desk*) To cover up your embarrassment.

In the distance, and getting nearer, the siren of an ambulance

Come on, Julia, the shindig must go on! Let's you and me get ourselves a stiff drink.

Liz and Julia go out L. *They leave the door open. Loud music from offstage*

Roz, in a rage, seizes the knife and spears the remaining balloon

Ambulance siren is now very near

Quick fade to Black-out

FURNITURE AND PROPERTY LIST

Scene 1

On stage: Four desks. *On each*: typewriter. *On 1:* telephone, mail including invoices. *On 2:* filing tray, notebook. *On 3:* pad of blank invoices. *In 4:* paper carbons, bottle of Martini
Four typists' chairs
Filing cabinet

Off stage: Filing tray containing papers (**Julia**)
Two letters (**Julia**)

Personal: **Kate:** watch

Scene 2

Set: *In desk 1:* 2 black polythene sacks. *On desk 2:* balloons, pump, tray of filing, rubber stamp, glasses, letter knife, deflated balloon. *On desk 3:* blown-up balloons

Off stage: Seven balloons strung together (**Roz**)
Envelope containing Christmas card (**Kate**)

Personal: **Barbara:** handbag. *In it:* half bottle of gin, Christmas card

LIGHTING PLOT

Property fittings required: nil
Interior. The same scene throughout

Scene 1

To open: general interior lighting

Cue 1   **Barbara** sits, looking concerned   (Page 15)
           Black-out

Scene 2

To open: general interior lighting

Cue 2   Ambulance siren is now very near   (Page 32)
           Black-out

EFFECTS PLOT

Cue 1	**Julia:** "I'm not worried." *Telephone*	(Page 11)
Cue 2	**Roz:** "... who encourages them." *Telephone*	(Page 13)
Cue 3	**Julia** enters L *Snatch of pop music*	(Page 23)
Cue 4	**Julia** exits L *Snatch of pop music*	(Page 24)
Cue 5	**Liz** exits L *Snatch of pop music*	(Page 24)
Cue 6	**Kate** enters L *Music*	(Page 24)
Cue 7	**Liz** enters L *Music and male baying voices*	(Page 26)
Cue 8	**Roz** and **Julia** enter L *Repeat cue 7*	(Page 26)
Cue 9	**Roz** exits L *Repeat cue 7*	(Page 27)

Cue 10	**Roz** enters L *Loud burst of music*	(Page 29)
Cue 11	**Liz:** "... to cover your embarrassment." *Ambulance siren*	(Page 31)
Cue 12	**Liz** and **Julia** exit L *Loud music*	(Page 32)
Cue 13	**Roz** spears the remaining balloon *Ambulance siren very near*	(Page 32)

www.ingramcontent.com/pod-product-compliance
Lightning Source LLC
Chambersburg PA
CBHW070453050426
42450CB00012B/3257